Shadows in the Cave

DAN M. KHANNA

Copyright © 2015 Dan M. Khanna

All rights reserved.

ISBN: 0692374949
ISBN-13: 978-0692374948

DEDICATION

To My Sisters

Urmila, Indrani and Sumedha

For their love, support, encouragement and always believing in me.

CONTENTS

Prologue – Plato's Cave

The Love Life	1
The Broken Pieces	2
I Dream of Dreams	4
The Facade of Marriage	5
Turn the Clock	6
Broken Heart	8
The Blows of Fate	9
The Sinking Ship	11
The End of the Road	12
The End of an Affair	14
The Last Throw	15
The Hermit	16
The Faceless Mirror	17
The Dawn of End	18
The Lost Dream	19
The Empty Bed	20
I Missed the Boat	21
There was Life Once	23
The Love of My Life	24
Life After Death	25
My Sister	26
The Greatest Sister	27
The Final Door	28
Threading the Needle	30
Together Yet Apart	32
God and I	33
An Ordinary Life	34
The Damaged Goods	36
The Final Chapter	37
Victory and Defeat	38
The Summer of Discontent	40
The Endless Struggle	42
The Race to Death	44

The Prisoner of Mistakes	45
Smoothing the Curves	46
Punishment and Penance	47
The Prisoner of Society	48
My Reflection on Me	49
An Angelic Child	50
The Train	52
Capsizing	53
The Cycle of Mistakes	54
The Demise of Life	55
My Life	56
Running Away	57
The Role Model	58
The End of the Line	59
The Fork in the Road	61
The Dreams	62
The Empty Playground	63
The Empty Tears	64
The Life I Missed	65
My Luck	66
In God's Hand	67
The Pungent Odor	68
The Emotional Roller Coaster	69
Lost in Life	70
Time to Leave	71
The Fateful Day	72
The Writing Dilemma	73
Life's Lessons	74
I Shouldn't Be Here	77
Time Was Not on My Side	78
Is God He or She?	79
The Materialistic Soul	80
The Spiritual Soul	81
The Foundation of Mistakes	82
Ripping the Heart	83
The Bleeding Stone	84
Not Near Enough	85
The Puppet of the Gods	86
The Curse of the Romantic	88

Peeling the Layers	90
Exist to Exist	91
The Last Chapter	92
Living on the Edge	93
An Unexamined Life	94
The Dice of Life	95
The Lonely Coffin	96
The Broken Pieces	97

PROLOGUE – PLATO'S CAVE

The allegory of Plato's Cave represents a cold environment where people lived their lives isolated from the outside world. They were comfortable with their shadows, interacted with each other and their own shadows and accepted their limited world as normal. They were afraid to venture out into the unknown world. They stayed within the walls of the cave while the world outside changed.

Today, most people live in a cave of their own making, comfortable with their environments and afraid to venture out.

It is our thinking that needs to change and our thoughts that need to expand and explore our changing world.

These poems explore the outside, the unknown.

Dan Khanna

THE LOVE LIFE

The love life!
What is it?
A life of love
Or, love of life.
I like life
But, do I love it?
Do I have to?
I did not choose my life
So, why should I love it?
But, then since I am in life
It is my life
I must love it
Why?
But, I can love
I can love life
If I want to
For loving is good
It feels good
But, it will be better
If I had a love
A love I could love
To make it
A real love life
A life of love
With the love of your life
Then you can love life
And life loves you
And that is
A love life.

THE BROKEN PIECES

The broken pieces
Shattered by the wind
Scatter among the sand
Dormant and still
I gave at it
What happened to the glass?
A clear crystalline fragile piece
Lying helpless
With no life.

I see it is not glass
It is my heart
That lies there
Broken into myriads of pieces
Dashed by the gale
That broke through
Its fragile strength
What do I do?

I feel a vacuum in my chest
That I must fill
With my heart
But how?
As I pick the pieces
How do I know
That I have all the pieces
I may never know

I scramble in the sand
Desperately picking up
Every piece that shines

I gather them
In a mud bowl
To put them together
Like a jigsaw puzzle
Do I have all the pieces?
Will I have the missing pieces?
What do I do with an incomplete heart?
Damaged and broken
What glue do I use?
Hope and faith
The builders of life
I see the structure evolve
A broken shape
But it is my heart
However incomplete
But, it is all I have
The remnants of a broken history
Struggling to be strong
To withstand
The next
Gust of wind.

I DREAM OF DREAMS

I dream of dreams
That I cannot have
I dream of love
That I cannot find
In this hollow world
Where love is a commodity
That is bought and sold.

I dream of life
That is quiet and tranquil
In a world that is full of turmoil
Killings and struggle.

I dream of a relationship
That is sincere and pure
In a selfish world.
I still dream
For dreams are real
It is future
It is hope.

THE FACADE OF MARRIAGE

Is marriage real?
Or, a facade
For the society
To show
That we are together
A man and a woman
In happy union
To avoid loneliness
Or, to feel complete as humans.

It is heaven
If it works
It is hell, when it doesn't
Marriage
Swinging
Between heaven and hell
Joy and pain
Hoping that
The union lasts forever
Whenever forever ends
The facade of marriage.

TURN THE CLOCK

If I could turn the clock back
Where will I start?
At birth.
To be born without a choice
In a world
That I knew nothing about.

Or should I turn it
To my first love
When I felt
The pangs of emotions
That illicit joy and pain
To carve a scar
That exists until today.

Or, should I go back
To a career
That I started
That I did not want
To live a life
That I did not cherish.

Or, should I go back
To the marriage
That I knew
Was doomed from the start
Yet I married
In the facade of the society
To lose everything
I had accumulated
Emptiness and alone.

Where do I go back?
Maybe not
For life is preordained
No clock decides the result
It's destiny
What is written happens
Clocks are for time
Time that clicks away
Projects us into the future.

BROKEN HEART

A broken heart
Is a rich heart
Full of experiences
Of happiness and sorrow
It knows pleasure
It knows pain
It is a happy heart
That is full of memories of love
It once had
And it once cherished
It is a proud heart
That knew how to love
How to feel the emotions
Of joy and completeness
It did not ask how it will end
For the heart is pure emotion
That thrives on love
Seeking its pleasure
And worried about pain
But, it does get broken
It is okay
It may never be complete
It may never be new
But, it is wiser
More contemplative
More experienced
More seasoned
It is an ancient tree
That has withstood
The onslaughts of seasons
But still stands erect

THE BLOWS OF FATE

The blows of fate
Come in all shapes and sizes
Some, a gentle nudge
That reminds us
That we are not doing
What we should
We tend to improve it
Our pride steps in the way
We ignore the gentle nudges
We move on.
Then comes a jolt
That knocks you off the pedestal
Reminding you
That you are so off track
Ignoring your life
That life sends a reminder
That you better
Get on your pedestal
And take charge of your life
Otherwise, you will feel the jolt again
To remind you that you are
A wayward traveler
Who has lost his path
And must get up
And follow your dream
Dreams that may inject
A jolt of electricity
To revive
What was once dead
To awaken a desire
That lay dormant

Under the sand
Waiting for the sand to scatter
And expose the real me
That I had buried within me
To shroud myself
From reality
On the onslaughts of fate
But, I need to expose myself
To life, to fate
Not, for its onslaught

But, to face its onslaught
Reflect its blows
To make a better world
For myself
Where the blows of fate
Don't torment me
Where I am my own blows
Blows that propel me upwards
To my dreams and fate.

THE SINKING SHIP

The sinking ship
Is a lucky ship
For it experiences its sinking
From floating
At the crest of waves
To the coolness
Of a calm bottom
It sees the horizon
At different depths
'Til it crosses a fine line
That forever sucks it
Into its watery bosom
A final resting place
Peace at last.

THE END OF THE ROAD

The road
That we travel
As we journey through life
Comes to an end
What do we do?
Just stop
Or, find another road
Or, build a new road.

Just stop
And admit it is over
You have done
The best you could do
And time has run out
It is time to quit
Just stop
And wait.

Or find another road
For it is not over for you
Another road
That allows you
To avoid mistakes
On the first road
Is there such a road?

Where do I find it?
Will it be the right road?
I don't know
Will I make the same mistakes?
Or make new mistakes
On a new road.

Or, should I build a new road
That erases the past
And takes me on a new journey
That builds a future
That I dreamed of
A simple life
Of love and happiness
Starting from scratch
With new hopes and faith
That, I am a changed person
A person who had lost his way
But now must correct the past
As he builds a new road
With new stones
A road that will never end
And continue through eternity.

THE END OF AN AFFAIR

It was great
While it lasted
Yes, it did have its moments
Pleasure and pain
Both exciting sensations
That grinds you in ecstasy
To propel you to the end of an affair
Full of memories
Both good and bad
Leaving us rich
In experiences and wisdom
To face the next affair
With dignity.

THE LAST THROW

The last throw of dice
On the gambling table of life
Is a daring challenge
Risking it all
On just one throw
To win or lose everything
The fate of life
Rests on this throw
Either walks away a winner
Or, a great loser
Sometimes
Life demands that of us
To risk it all
In a last throw.

THE HERMIT

The hermit sits alone
Meditating
Trying to find answers to life
That continue to elude him
He is alone
But, not alone
For within him
Is the wisdom of the ages
That holds him together
Life and death have no meaning for him
For they are two sides
Of the same existence
He is content in both
For he has balanced
Both life and death
That are within him
Existing together
In a tight embrace
Celebrating the joys of togetherness
Of eternal love
He is at peace
For he is the hermit.

THE FACELESS MIRROR

I see the mirror
But I can't see myself
I see a shadow
That is struggling
To come alive
I reach out
Touch the mirror
Trying to shake myself
To see myself
But, I don't see myself
I see the emptiness
That was once me
Just a reflection
That is not me
Emptiness
Where my face should have been
Is just a mirror
A faceless mirror.

THE DAWN OF END

I am staring
At a brilliant dawn
Orange reddish
Rays streaming
Through the distant mountains
Bringing color
To scattered clouds
It is beautiful
Another day of hope
A new day
That tells me
That it is the start
Of my end
Ending a journey
That began at birth
It is the dawn of the end
It is so beautiful
Exhilarating and thrilling
I now know
That twilight will come
With the sunset
As the golden sun
Plunges into the ocean
Scattering the sky
With brilliant colors.

Will my end be like that?
Showering colors at the world
Or will my sun
Drown behind the clouds
For no one to see
Or experience my end
Just an end
That no one saw
But, the dawn was beautiful
It started the end
A glorious end.

THE LOST DREAM

There was once a dream
Of a life
Of happiness, love and peace
Of togetherness
With the one you love
Sharing intimacy and emotions
But, then dreams are just dreams
Not reality
Just and hope
And faith in life
As I stand alone
Facing the facing
In an empty world
Still hoping
Still dreaming
Hoping to capture
The lost dream.

THE EMPTY BED

I reach across the bed
Searching for you
It is middle of the night
It is cold and lonely
I search for warmth
A touch
Just to feel
That there is you
There on the other side of the bed
But, the space is empty
A cold mattress
I grope
Hands and fingers
Hoping for a body
'Til it dawns on me
That I am alone in bed
I cry silently
Lamenting at an empty bed.

I MISSED THE BOAT

I stand on the shores
Of the river
Waving at the boat
That was to carry me
To a distant land.
I missed it again
I miss it all the time
The burdens of life
Derail me
I always arrive late
Haunted and hunted
By the daily existence
That thwarts my future journey
Yet I must come every day
Try to board
The boat
That will take me
To a new world
Where I can begin again
To make a world
That I couldn't on this shore
To make a new life
That excludes the mistakes
Of the present.
But, first I must
Show up on time
To let go of past
To be here
When the boat leaves

To board it
With all my belongings
And sail down the river
To a new shore
For a new beginning.

THERE WAS LIFE ONCE

There was a life once
In this fragile body
A promising life
Full of hope of success
It was successful
Joy, love, security, contentment
All the right ingredients
It was life
Living up to its
Full glamour and exuberance
Then came an earthquake
Followed by a tidal wave
It dashed hopes
Leveled the lofty ideals
Into dusty particles
That kept scattering
In the wind
Far away
So there was nothing
To gather
Except a dream
A dream of life
That is lost forever.

THE LOVE OF MY LIFE

The love of my life
Is missing
In flesh and touch
But remains in my heart
As a love
Carved in my heart
And that is
The love of my life.

LIFE AFTER DEATH

Life after death
Is beautiful
Surrounded by natural beauty
In a loving world
Where all are equal
Affectionate and loving
It is a peaceful world
Where hopes and faith abound
An eternal resting place
For our soul
A place to live quietly
And to be one
With God.

MY SISTER

My eldest sister
Was a gem of love
Generously giving
Love, affection, understanding
Unselfish
Not wanting anything for herself
Remained simple
Like a saint
Loved and respected by all
She left a legacy
Of giving and caring
Ideals that we must all strive for
I am proud and privileged
She was my sister
And, I was her
Little brother.

THE GREATEST SISTER

My eldest sister
Is the greatest sister
One can ever have
I was her doll
She loved and protected me
With affection
She showered me
With caring wisdom
She bathed me
She dressed me
So I could look
Pretty and cute
She got me ready everyday
To get me to school
As a friend
She guided me in life
So I could become
A better person
We shared
Our loves, our music, our thoughts
Evenings and nights
Indulging in crying emotions
And sharing feelings
Those were just between us
She enriched my life
Beyond even my parents
To her, I was her baby
A kid brother
That loved her.

She is no longer physically present
But she is in my heart and soul
I hope to meet her some day
In a better world
And continue
Our journey together.

THE FINAL DOOR

Doors open
Doors close
Life goes through doors
Some open by themselves
Some you try to open
Some are hard to open
Some you pry open
And, some never open.

Life is a series of doors
We must understand
What doors mean?
The ones that are forever closed
Should we pry them open?
Or, just go to another door
Maybe, that door
Is not meant for us
Maybe, it is a divine message
Let that door remain closed
Do not force it
For you may not
Like what you see
Some doors
You must open by yourself
These doors are part of your journey
They need your energy
Your will
And your determination
To move forward.

And then there are doors
That just open by themselves
You are scared
Why did it open?
Are you supposed to go through it?
What will you see on the other side?

Unknown haze awaits you
The light is inviting.
You feel good
Go through that door
It is your destiny
It is divine trust
For the door was opened for you
Take it
And then

There is a final door
We come to the end of doors
Only one last door remains
This door we must pass through
It is not a choice
It is final
This door takes us
Into a new world
Where we are one
With the universe
It is
The final door.

THREADING THE NEEDLE

Threading the needle
Is an art
That I have not mastered
I can see the hole in the needle
I hold the thread in my hand
But when they come together
My hand shakes
I miss
Again and again
I steady myself
Thin the thread
Still I miss
I wish the hole were bigger
But the mirage
Keeps separating the alignment
I miss again and again
Just like my life
I can see it
But, I keep passing it by
So close
Yet so far
I see it
And I don't see it
Like my life
Happiness and living
Is life
Trying to thread
Happiness through life
But, it just misses
Again and again

So I begin again
With hope and confidence
Trying to thread the needle again.

TOGETHER YET APART

I see you in my heart
The throbbing of life
In my veins
Is you
For you are my life
I feel you in me
And then I look around
And don't see you
I am alone
With no one to touch
Just a memory of a love
Within me
But, no one to hold
We are together through eternity
But apart forever.

GOD AND I

God and I
Have a lovely relationship
He loves me
Protects me
Whenever I do something stupid
Yet He pounds me
When I do wrong
I like it that way
For I do love God
I know
I cannot do without Him
I remember
When I was down
He picked me up
When I was about to have an accident
He came to save me
A guardian angel
I know it was God
For only divine intervention
Could have protected me
The fatal illnesses
He carried me
Safely to safety
Yet, I question Him
Why am I here?
He tells me
You are my child
I love you
You will remain with Me
Forever
For I am your true friend
Who loves you unselfishly
Making you a better person
For you are Mine.

AN ORDINARY LIFE

I lead
A very ordinary life
I go to work
In a mediocre line of work
Pay the bills
Watch television and movies
For entertainment
See few friends occasionally
I cook to survive
I pay my taxes
Help government
Off my back
I vote most of the time
As a good citizen
To participate
In our political process
Knowing well
That it does not matter
What I vote
What I think
I am a non-entity
Just an ordinary citizen
Who makes this country run
It may be a boring life
But because of me
And many other ordinary citizens
This country is great
For we do our duty
We do our work
We know that our names
May not appear in local obituaries
But, that does not matter

For we made this country run
And made it a better place
We are simple
We are ordinary
Our lives are ordinary
But, we are special.

THE DAMAGED GOODS

The box
Sitting alone
Dented and damaged
Sides caved in
From transit
A lonely journey
It endured to reach its destination.

The box is me
Damaged goods
Scarred by life
Dented by emotions
Damaged by the world
As I tried to reach my destination.

Now I sit alone
Waiting for inspection
To see the extent of real damage
To fix what is broken
Or just pay out the insurance
But, I am damaged
Never to be whole again
Never to be perfect
I have to live with my fate
And accept the damage
Do what I can to continue my journey
Broken, but not defeated
For I am still a box
That contains me
I may be damaged
But, I am still alive.

THE FINAL CHAPTER

The book of life
Is about to end
The final chapter
Has to be written
How will it end?
A happy ending
Or, a sad ending
Or, an ending
That just ends.

How was the book?
Entertaining
Adventurous
Or just plain living
That ended
With no final chapter
But, there must be an end
A closure
That ends forever.

VICTORY AND DEFEAT

I win, I lose
My life stares at me
Wondering, what am I doing?
Peeking at the past
Or, gazing at the future
Even I don't know
What I am doing?
I have been a victor
I have been defeated
The ups and downs of life
Have eroded the differences
Between victory and defeat
To me now
They are two sides
Of the same coin
The lashings of life
Have welted my skin
To the point
That it has hardened
Into a protective covering
That makes victory or defeats the same
I can't tell the difference
The emotional exuberance
Is the same
The thrill is the same
The agony is the same
In one sense
It is just my life
A life of undulating curves
That propels forward
At uneven speeds
To jolt me

And remind me
That victory and defeat
Are the same.

THE SUMMER OF DISCONTENT

The time has come
To think of my life
As it nears a final closure
I wonder
Where am I?
What have I done?
It is a time for reflection
This summer
The summer of discontent
The restlessness
That permeates through me
The time has come
To rethink my life
And move to a new world
Where my past hopes
Will flourish
Where my lost dreams
Will be realized
Where I will find a home
My soul
And final resting place.
Where that is
I don't know
When will it happen?
I don't know
But, I know
That my time now
Has come to an end
Life and love
Are at crossroads
The past not very kind

The future
Beckons with open arms
To embrace me
In its bosom
To soothe me
To nurture my wounds
And bask me
In love and glory
And lay my head
In the pillow of God
Where I find myself
One with God
The finality to a life
That went astray
And must seek
Its end
In the palms
Of God.

THE ENDLESS STRUGGLE

The endless struggle with life
Goes on
What I want to be?
And what will life forces me to become?
What do I do?
Live in conflict
Or, cease to live
For what is living
In eternal turmoil
It splits the mind
And shatters all hope
The squandered opportunities
The love miscalculations
The career missteps
The financial failures
The list goes on
Of follies
The mountain of mistakes
The well of sins
Overflowing
Reminding me of the gutter
That I unleashed on myself
Drowning myself in my own vomit
Gasping for breath
In foul air
That corrupts the soul
And slowly chips away
At the decaying body
Alive but listless

To be slowly beaten up
By insects and maggots
To feel a world
That feeds on life
And makes life a struggle.

THE RACE TO DEATH

It is a race
Whether death will get me first
Or, I will get done what I want to
Who will win?
I don't know
Each day
Death draws me closer
To its bosom
And each day
I pull back
Trying to stretch my days
So I can complete the tasks
That I was sent for in this world
I may not know
What the tasks are
But, I feel
That I am not done yet in life
The struggle goes on
The yearning for the end
And pushing the end
To the end I want
It is a race
A race that will end someday
Who will win
I don't know
But, it is a race
That will end
With end.

THE PRISONER OF MISTAKES

As I gaze at the four walls
That imprison me
I wonder how I got here
A self-imposed, self-created prison
Built by my mistakes
That traveled with me
Throughout my life
Adding a brick
At every step
Earlier, I could walk on the bricks
Then I could leap over them
Soon the bricks became a wall
That slowly burst around me
And surrounded me
Leaving no space to escape
Except stare at the sky
Hoping for a miracle
But my hesitation
Soon covered the ceiling
And all I could see
Was my own self
Staring at me
Wondering
Why I imprisoned myself
In my own prison
There is no door
Breathing my own breath
Which gets polluted
With each breath
And soon there is no air
Just a vacuum
Enclosed by six walls
Making my life
A tomb
Of the living dead.

SMOOTHING THE CURVES

The curves and creases
Need smoothing
Try iron and press
Yet the marks remain
Refusing to go
Holding resolutely
To the clinks
Refusing to be straight and smooth
For what is there in smoothness
Just a flat surface
With no visible individuality
That no one can distinguish
What is that life?
That no one can identify
The curves are individual identity
That no one shall smooth
For smoothness destroys life
Makes us ordinary.

PUNISHMENT AND PENANCE

I kneel with bare chest
And exposed back
Waiting for the whip
To slash my back
And inflict stinging blow
Causing excruciating pain
And permanent marks
Marks of penance
And punishment for the sins
That I committed against my own life
A life that was ready for greatness
Yet, I fed it ignorance, stupidity and impulsiveness
Placing it in a gutter
Self-pity and remorse
For which I must pay
For my mistakes
The punishment
Too mild
The penance forever
As I get whipped
With the wounds of fate
Slashing and carving
My life
For a lesson
To the rest of humanity
Those mistakes get punished
And lessons have to be learned
And penance is divine
The ultimate truth
One with self.

THE PRISONER OF SOCIETY

The world is a prison
We leave only on death
The society is our prison
Telling us what to do
Telling us what to think
To create living robots
Draped in mediocrity
Living uneventful lives
And hoping
That we will be mentioned
In our local obituary
That our society values
Only few make it there
The rest just pass
Into a better world
Escaping a society
That is just a prison.

MY REFLECTION ON ME

My reflection on me
Is not very good
I may be nice
But who am I?
Even I don't know
I keep searching within me
And sometimes
I touch the edges
That may expose me
But my hands pull away
Afraid to gnaw at the shell
Afraid to crack it
And see what is inside
An infant
In a fetal position
Afraid to look up
Outside my shell
Peek at a world
That I don't know
So I remain motionless
In a moving world
Waiting for the right world
That will come and open doors for me
A world where I belong
And that is my reflection.

AN ANGELIC CHILD

The baby
Nine months old
Staring at my face
Clutching my finger
To draw me to her lips
To suck the love
That flows through it
The curly long hair
Flowing like a mane
Of a lion
Rich in glory
Shining with pride
The angel's smile
The agility of a deer
Running through life
Chasing dreams
Jumping in my arms
The warm embrace
Cuddling with joy
Following me with pride
To games and adventures
Listening to music
Sharing art and culture
Good and bad
Sadness and happiness
Growing together
In distant lands
Sharing tears and laughter
The music of our souls
As she grew to be
A god's child

Full of love and warmth
A heart immense as universe
A child
Now a woman
My daughter.

THE TRAIN

The train
Supported by two rails
Hurtles towards its destination
Hoping that the two tracks
Remain in place
And do not meet.

The train moves
Wishing that the tracks
Will lead it to its destination
For it cannot turn around
Once it starts
Sometimes the train
Embarks
On a different track
And winds up
In a direction
Where it was
Not meant to be
A path that is difficult
To retract
And winds up
At unknown destination
Where strangers greet you
And you make the best of journey
A false smile
Confused and confounded
Meeting strangers
Who wonder why you are there
You wonder why I am here.
A union of unknowns.

CAPSIZING

The boat
That is afloat
Sailing on scary water
That supports it
Springs a leak
A slow leak
The water that held it
Now into its bosom
Slowly sinking it
Engulfing in its embrace
As the boat sinks to the bottom
A floor to support it
In its final resting place
It is finally over.

THE CYCLE OF MISTAKES

The cycle of mistakes
Takes a toll on life
With every step
That moves you ahead
The jolt of mistakes
Pushes it backwards two steps
The unending struggle
To move forward
Is pushed back
By every mistake
I make in my path
One step forward
Two steps backward
I cannot even reach
Where I started
Now the start
Is merely a goal
To get back
To where I can start fresh
To break
The cycle of mistakes.

THE DEMISE OF LIFE

When does life end?
Not with death
For death is just a lifeless entity
Of a human body
That just ceased to move
But, life could have ended
While living
It could have ended
When one decides it is over
Or one has done
All one can do
The limits are attained
There is not much to do
Life becomes a mere existence
Just a survival
That is the demise of life.

MY LIFE

My life is an open book
You open it
Read the first page
And then close it
Everything is in it
But nothing is in it
Just empty pages
Staring blankly
Waiting for substance
Some writing
That would brighten up the pages
But nothing appears
The invisible ink
Writes about me
That I only can see
It is my life
Only I knew
If I really knew.

RUNNING AWAY

I want to run away
From myself
But, I can't
For myself does not leave me
It hugs me
Scared
To be left behind
It does not let me go
I push it
I shove it
It clings even holding me tightly
To endure my life
That I am running away from
The thorns stick
Hurt
But, I try to pull away
But, it is fruitless
For life has embraced me
I am part of it
I am it
I have to live with it
It is me
It is my life
I own it
For, I cannot
Run away from it.

THE ROLE MODEL

Am I a role model to myself?
What can I learn from myself?
Yes, I have
Plenty to teach myself
I am a role model to myself
I have learned
That I am average
Prone to errors and mistakes
I make mistakes
Many
And then I live correcting them
That is my life
Make mistakes
Learn
Correct them
And then make more mistakes
I am, indeed, a role model
To myself.

THE END OF THE LINE

The train stops
It is the last station
It is the end of the line
I have to get off
I have no choice
I want to go further
But, I can't
I wonder what I will see
When I get off
Has my journey stopped?
Journeys of life
Do not stop
They halt
Or get derailed
But, do not stop
I have to leave the train
I step out of the train
Seeking exit
To a place that I don't know
Searching for a familiar face
To give me direction
But, I am alone
All directions
Seem the same to me
They all lead everywhere and nowhere
With just my instinct and destiny
To guide me
I venture out
To bright sunshine
Amidst strangers
To search for a new train

That will continue my journey
To unknown destination
'Til it comes
To the end of its line.

THE FORK IN THE ROAD

The crossroads of life
Stands empty
Desolate and barren
I stand alone
Beaten by hot desert wind
What to do?
Where to go?
So many paths
Leading in so many directions
All shrouded with dust
With no visible end
I have to move
I have to travel
Pick a road
I seek
Heavenly guidance
None is there
I toss my fate to the winds
And take a road
Not knowing where it will go
Where it will end
But, I must travel as life demands
And trust fate
My past determines my future
I am on a path
That will determine my future
My destiny
I must accept.

THE DREAMS

The dreams
Come and go
Awakening my soul
Showing images of my life
That I don't see in real life
Pictures of people
Who love and hate me
That I have never met
Parents, who still bless me from heaven
Bestowing love and affection
I reach out to touch them
But, they are gone
Leaving love and blessings
To their wayward son
I dream of
Places, I have never seen
Wandering to find
A monument that I know
I dream of
Situations
Where I am lost
I keep searching
Not finding what I want
The search ends
I am awake
I still grope the reality
To see where I am
But not where I want to be
The dream is over
I am still here
Dreaming.

THE EMPTY PLAYGROUND

I want to play
Games of life
I seek a playground
Where I can play with playmates
But, the playground is empty
I am there alone
I search for games
For playmates
I just hear
An eerie silence
The games are empty
Desolate and lonely
I play alone
Winning and losing
With myself
Each game reminds me
That this playground of life
Is an empty one for me
I will play
But alone
I will win
But alone
I will lose
But alone
This playground
Will eventually shut down
And I will have no place to go
I will remain empty.

THE EMPTY TEARS

The tears
Trickle down the cheeks
Burning the skin
With hurt and pain
Of a life
Longing for itself
They fall on empty earth
Watering the plants
That died years ago
Burning a hole in the ground
That buried the soul
Of a true lover
Yet the tears flow
Washing the scars
That life and people have marked
On the grave
Keeping it clean
For prayers about life
That left years ago
But the tears must flow
To cleanse the soul
Of sins
That I never committed
Just a watery grave
Of empty tears.

THE LIFE I MISSED

I once had a life
It was beautiful
With loving parents and family
I grew up
The parents
Flew into a better world
While I stood
On a strange planet
Alone and unloved
The loves come
Scratching my heart
Carving wounds
Leaving scars
That would design my life
A life longing for love
That would elude me
Throughout my life
I miss the friendships
That brought us together
Then scattered us
Throughout the world
Leaving memories of a life
That should have been mine
But, I got off
At the wrong time
And I missed life
Forever.

MY LUCK

My luck expired
Sometime during my early years
And the life became a struggle
Surviving daily for the next day
Leaving dreams behind
Creating new dreams
Seeing them crash against the rocks
Just like my luck
Beating on empty hopes
It is not just my life
My luck deserted me
A long time ago.

IN GOD'S HAND

The Hand of God
Holds me gently
Keeping me warm and comfortable
I am contented
I live a life
That pulls me in all directions
I don't know what to do
My plans don't work
My dreams crash
I just give up
Lost and confused
Then I look up
Seeking Divine guidance
That will hold my life
And guide me wisely
To whatever destination
God desires
I let myself go
I have to
For I have not done
A great job with my life
And I put myself
In God's Hand.

THE PUNGENT ODOR

The pungent odor
Oozes from the earth
That supports humans
Who scourge the planet
With lies, deceit and killings
Of fellow humans
Emanating a foul odor of death
That envelops the planet
And suffocating its inhabitants
With the stench of decay
Creating a pungent odor.

THE EMOTIONAL ROLLER COASTER

One moment
She is here
Other moment
She is gone
One moment she loves me
Other moment
She is not sure
One moment
She wants to spend her life with me
Other moment
She says she is not sure
The ups and down of emotions
Bring joy and pain
Just like a roller coaster
Of emotions.

LOST IN LIFE

I am lost in life
Don't know what to do
Emptiness
Surrounds me
Helplessness overwhelms me
I reach out touching nothing
Feeling nothing in the darkness
Groping for hope
In a hopeless world
Nothing to hold
Just faith
And a desire
That life
Will become life.

TIME TO LEAVE

There comes a time in life
When one realizes
That it is time to leave
One has done
What one can do
It may not have been pretty
But, it was once a reality
But, it is over
There is nothing much to do
I have done what I could have done
There is nothing more to do
Just existing to survive
Is a curse of death
To end life
When it is over
You did what you could
Accept the judgment
That it is over
It is time
Time to leave.

THE FATEFUL DAY

The day
The fateful day
Has arrived
I have to go to a better world
Or to a world
Where I have to live
My life all over again
Do I have a choice?
Or my choice is already made for me
Should I fight?
Or, just let it go
Shall I try to change the outcome?
Or, accept it
As part of fate
The divine destiny
Do I have a say?
The day is here
I stand alone
Seeing everything
And seeing nothing
Just an invisible universe
Calling me to float
'Til I feel nothing
'Til I pass into world
That is not a world
It is just me
Devoid of me
That fateful day.

THE WRITING DILEMMA

Writing
Cleansing of the soul
Happens in spurts
And then
There is a lull
When nothing comes out
You want to write
But don't or can't
The mind is dead
The feelings are numb
The urge is strong
But, no words come out
The paper is blank
The pen is dry
The eyes scan the page
Writing with invisible ink
The turbulent thoughts
The fluctuating feelings
Giving it words
That others can see
And feel the feelings
That explode with expression
To silence the soul
That is sailing
In turbulent waters
The writing
Bringing life to words
Is what writers do
Like to do
When to do
That is the writer's dilemma.

LIFE'S LESSONS

My life
What have I learned from it
As I enter the twilight of my life?

I reflect
The memories take me back
To my carefree youth
Under the love and guidance of my parents.

Then I was on my own
Living an adventurous life
Traveling through spaces
And strange lands
Searching for a dream
I may or may not find
The undulating plains
Throwing me up and down
Catching me
Propelling me up again
Holding me
When I fell
But, it was a good life
Will I change anything?
No
It was meant for me
And I have lived it with emotion
Good and bad
Happy and sad
Just like any other life
But, it was mine
As I see the end
I leave my thoughts
Of the lessons that I learned.

First, plans do not always work
Plan, but do not live by it
The frustration and disillusionment
May shatter your will
For will is strong
And you must have it
To endure your journey.

Second, not everything in life
Can be explained
Some things just happen
Some people we just meet
Some events just happen
Some episodes just appear
Accept it
Let it go
Do not analyze
Do not question
Do not question!
Just accept it
As a divine gift
That is what we are given
It is our path
Just learn and move on.

Third, our minds become destructive
It fails to reason
It shuts up
Justifying every thought and action
Our mind has taken over
We have exited our soul
We live in an artificial world
Leaving touch with reality
That is self-destructive.

Fourth, we must bear the responsibility of our decisions
Our actions
Not blame others
Not blame the system
Not blame life

Accept the consequences
Of your decisions
Learn to live with you
It is all you have
It will make you an emotionally richer human.

These are the lessons I share with the world around me
As I fade into oblivion
My life is lived
But the journey continues.

I SHOULDN'T BE HERE

I shouldn't be here
In this place
In this world
I am here
Not knowing why I am here
I go through the motions
Of living and surviving
Wondering why do I wake up
And do as most of the world does
Trying to make a living
To take care of our responsibilities
And then sleep at night
To rest and regroup
To do the same thing all over again
And then we die
And search for our obituary
If it shows up
And then we realize
That we just lived
Why and where
But we are here
Life goes on
We remain a speck
That no one sees
That is life.

TIME WAS NOT ON MY SIDE

Time is running out
I can see the peaceful space
That is waiting for me
I can feel
The colorful shroud
That will cover me
Embrace me
As it delves me in God's hand
But, my time is not over
I still have unfulfilled dreams
Things I have not done
Lives that I have not lived
Feelings that I have not felt
Love that I have not loved
But, I must go
I can't push the end
But, I can make the end wait
'Til I feel I am ready
Time is not on my side
But, time is what I have
It is my time
And 'til that end
Time is my friend
I have to live
And prolong the end
'Til I am ready
Time is me.

IS GOD HE OR SHE?

God is male
God is a female
But that is wrong
God is both
God does not choose sex
For God is God
But I can say
God is both
When He smites us
Punishes us
It is He - a male
When it nurtures us
Love us
Supports us
It is She - a female
It is my God
No matter
What it is.

THE MATERIALISTIC WORLD

I had a soul
A good soul
A spiritual soul
That I sold for
Worldly pleasures
A materialistic life
Of goods and comforts
That separated me from me
I was two individuals
Living in one body
One struggling to embrace life
The other struggling to devour life
The short-term gratifications
Makes each day easy to live
Pleasures that let day go by
Then one day you realize
That it was an empty life
There was no soul
Just an existence
Surrounded by materialism
Searching for answers
That will forever elude me
For I lived in a materialistic world
I became
A materialistic soul.

THE SPIRITUAL SOUL

My soul
That travels in my body
Is an ancient soul
That lives in a spiritual world
In unity with God
To accumulate
All the wisdom of the universe
But, we don't see it
It is old
It is new
It is timeless
It is the essence of life
That carries us
Through storms and earthquakes
For it is aligned with God
It carries His blessings
His love for me
And guides me to paths
That is cleared for me
To continue my journey
With the spirit of God
With His name on my lips
And that is
The spiritual soul.

THE FOUNDATION OF MISTAKES

My life is built
On foundations of mistakes
Each mistake
Laying layers
That gradually
Creep up building a pyramid
That entombs me
Into a shrine
From which
I cannot come out
Lying peacefully
In a cold dark world
Staring
At the monument of mistakes.

RIPPING THE HEART

You ripped my heart
You shredded it to pieces
And scattered them into the wind
For vultures to feed on it
Why?
Is heart just a feeding ground
Where you pick and prod
Picking the pieces you like
Discarding pieces
That do not taste well
But, the heart is a soul
One piece that should remain intact
Should remain intact
Not meant to be ripped
And squandered to the wind
But the pieces of heart
Gather in the dust
Assemble and unite
To form a sacred structure
With deep wounds
To remind you
That it is still a heart
One heart
Damaged but together
Struggling to breathe
Life into a dying soul
It is a heart
The only heart.

THE BLEEDING STONE

The stone
That bleeds tears
Is my heart
A pulsating emotion
That crashed into a meteorite
Instantly turning into a molten stone
That bleeds at will
As it gets kicked and thrown
To fall with pain
On a cruel surface
Shrieking a silent scream
That no one hears
It sits alone
Waiting for the next kick
Waiting for someone
To pick up
And throw far away
To be picked up again
Maybe, the stone is unique
It has a personality
That someone will hold it
Caress it
And take it
For a collector item
To sit alone
Among other stones
Reflecting how it got there
Bleeding tears
Of joy and sorrow
Staying still
In perpetual stillness
To be forgotten forever.

NOT NEAR ENOUGH

It is near
I can see it
I can feel it
But, it is not near enough
Where I can touch it
And be in it
I still have to do many things
To bridge the gap
The things that I should have done
But let the sands of time
Derail it
Now as I approach near
Time is short
An enemy
But I have to do it
For near is not still near.

THE PUPPET OF THE GODS

Gods created a puppet
A human
That they can play with
They can make him
Whatever they want
A fun game
Even gods need fun
I am the puppet
That gods created for amusement
An entertaining caricature
Of a divine soul
They gave me a smart brain
Then make sure
That I don't use it well
I flounder and stumble
They cheer when I stumble
They applaud when I get up
I take the blows
I rock back and forth
Trying to stay stable
And go on with my dance
To amuse them
They pull the strings
They pull the strings
They give me joy
I laugh
They drop me
I hurt
I cry
They pick me up
Make me dance
They laugh
'Til their laughter brings tears
Then they drop me
They see me crying with pain
They feel sorry

They pick me up
Pull my strings
And ask me to dance to their joy
The cycle goes on
I remain a puppet
At the strings of God
Just a puppet.

THE CURSE OF THE ROMANTIC

I am romantic
I love romance
I want to love
Experience the feeling
The butterfly youth
I am ready to endure
And the pain that may come with it
But the joy
When you find love
Overshadows the hurt
But romance is an illusion
That reality shatters
For romance is a curse
It only brings expectations
Desires that remain unfulfilled
But still remain
Tug of war
Being pulled in two directions
Pulling you apart
Tormenting with pain
That spreads through you
Sending jolts of lightening
Through your body
You can't laugh
You can't cry
Laughter is hurting
Tears are stones
That just stay there
Romance is a curse
You want it
You don't want it
That is the paradox
You live with the duality

An eternal struggle
That remains with you
'Til you die
That is the curse of the romantic.

PEELING THE LAYERS

Life is built by layers
Each layer enveloping an experience
That we go through
As we build our lives
Each layer shrouds us
Gives us a new experience
That shapes our perceptions of ourselves
Soon we are nothing except layers of life
That hide us
From our true selves
Then one day we look at ourselves in the mirror
And not see us
Just layers that cover us
We are aliens to ourselves
We start peeling the layers
One layer at a time
Slowly but surely
Not ready to shock ourselves
As layers come off
Just like a mask
The experiences come off
Exposing our real self
The innocent self
That created life and God
Trying to find the love of life
That was divine
But got covered with layers
The peeling goes on
'Til we are naked and done
All divine, all human
Our true self.

EXIST TO EXIST

I live
Actually I exist
I go through the motions of life
I go to work
Where it is just work
To get paid
So I can take care of basic needs
Yes, I have desires
But my meager sustenance
Negates any desires
Yes, I have dreams
But they remain dreams
For existence takes all energy away
I become a robot
Going through the motions
Of living each day
Bringing me closer to the end
Wondering is this all to life
Oh, yes
I wanted more
But the hurricanes of life
Leveled all hopes
The loves vanished
'Til life became mere existence
Now I exist to exist.

THE LAST CHAPTER

The last chapter
Is the end of the story
But does story ever end
The end of every story starts another story
The last chapter is really a beginning
Of a new story
For a story is just an episode of life
That puts on paper
What one feels
They are just words
To the rhythm of life
Connected but disconnected
The chapter may end
But the story continues.

LIVING ON THE EDGE

I stand at the edge of a cliff
A deep ravine gaping at me
It is daunting
It is tempting
Do I take a step forward?
And plunge into emptiness
Or should I step back to safer ground?
The choice is mine
Somehow I wish
A gust of wind
Would push me
And then I take my chances with fate
Do I crash?
Or, do I survive?
Living on the edge
Is a thrill
A challenge
That I must face
To plunge into a better world
Or hold on to familiar ground
Where much of life is wasted
Or, jump into a free world
And let destiny guide.

AN UNEXAMINED LIFE

An unexamined life
Is not worth living
As a great philosopher once said
But to examine a life
That was not worth living
Is even more painful
Yes, we do examine our life
As it goes through stages
Of learning and living
Examining from our own perspective
What we got
What we did not get
To examine is to probe our soul
An untouched and unblemished
Part of us
That is divine
What do we get?
When we examine ourselves
Demons and ghosts
Angels and blessings
Our mind is warped
By the vagaries of living
To examine ourselves
Is to examine our mind
To give us answers
That we crave
It is best
To let life go unexamined
For living is an art
Just do it.

THE DICE OF LIFE

Life is a gamble
We are dealt cards
That we need to live with
We throw dice
Hoping to win
But, it is a chance
We gamble our lives
On opportunities and hope
Dreaming of dreams
Throwing dice with the hope
That it will be the last throw

You bet it all
Pray, and throw the dice
You close your eyes
To make a final wish
It will be all or nothing
You will get what you want
Or walk away alone and lonely
As an empty loser
But, one must try
To test fate
And bet it all
On one throw
The last dice of life.

THE LONELY COFFIN

Lying alone
In a cold coffin
Is scary and sad
Nicely dressed
People staring at you
But you cannot respond
You just lie there
Awaiting the final journey
To the bosom of the earth
Surrounded by dirt and worms
A fitting end to a life
That started alone
And ended alone.

THE BROKEN PIECES

The broken pieces
Lie scattered on the floor
They were all together once
Sculpted and in harmony
Enjoying beauty and peace
But, eternity is a hope
Hopes to get shattered
And now the pieces lay apart
Thinking if they will ever be one
Will they ever join
To form a beautiful sculpture
Or just remain on the ground
To be swept away
Into the dust.

ABOUT THE AUTHOR

Dan Khanna considers himself a traveler through life enjoying an adventurous journey. Dan was born in New Delhi, India. After he completed high school, at St. Columbus High School, Dan left India striking out for California via short stays in London, Montreal and Milwaukee, Wisconsin. Although his dream was to pursue a career in the arts, acting, music, and writing, a quirk of fate placed him in engineering college and pursuing a business management career, in which he excelled. Dan completed an undergraduate program in engineering, and a Master and Doctorate in Business Administration.

Dan worked in Silicon Valley's high technology firms and was a CEO and founder of several firms. He changed careers to be a professor. Now, he again is pursuing his dream in creative endeavors.

Dan is the quintessential Renaissance Man, whose interests span the gamut of the arts, sciences, history, social and political studies, classics and philosophy. His search for knowledge began in his early life where his father was the Chief Education Officer of Delhi and his mother was a Sanskrit scholar. Dan speaks English, Hindi, Urdu, Punjabi, and Gujarati.

As a child, Dan read voraciously, particularly enjoying novels, such as Sherlock Holmes, Agatha Christie, Earl Stanley Gardener, Ian Fleming's James Bond series and classic works of Shakespeare, Tolstoy, Dickens, Oscar Wilde, Thomas Hardy, and other writers. He was very interested in poetry and read English poems of Browning, Keats, Milton, Tennyson, and Frost, as well as, other poets, while mastering Urdu poetry. His intellectual interests including studying Western and Eastern philosophers, especially Socrates, from whom he learned questioning methodology employed in his research, lectures and seminars.

During his parochial education, Dan was interested in various sports: cricket, soccer and field hockey. His love for the arts and music was honed to a level that he performed in plays, movies and solo concerts.

Dan's present journey is devoted to creative arts and activities, primarily writing poetry, fiction and non-fiction books and plays, while continuing to acquire knowledge of diverse subjects. He has published one book and has written over twelve hundred poems comprising nineteen books to date. Dan has several non-fiction and fiction books in development.